FUN BIBLE SUDOKU

50+ PUZZLES WITH A TRIVIA TWIST!

BARBOUR PUBLISHING

Published by Barbour Publishing, Inc., 1810 Barbour Drive, Uhrichsville, Ohio 44683 www.barbourbooks.com

Our mission is to inspire the world with the life-changing message of the Bible.

 Member of the
Evangelical Christian
Publishers Association

Printed in the United States of America.

WELCOME
to the world of
BIBLE SUDOKU!

Millions worldwide have discovered the joy of sudoku—the puzzle that tests your skills of logic. The rapid growth in sudoku's popularity has rightly been called a phenomenon.

But what in the world is "Bible sudoku"? We're glad you asked!

Fun Bible Sudoku combines the enjoyment of solving a sudoku puzzle with the challenge of Bible trivia. First, you put your Bible knowledge to the test, answering scripture-based questions to determine either the numerical or letter-based "givens" for each puzzle. Then you prove your logic abilities by completing the sudoku grid.

Here's how it works exactly:

NUMBER-BASED PUZZLES

1. Each puzzle begins with a blank 9 x 9 grid. A coordinate system—with the letters A through I across the top and the numbers 1 through 9 down the left side—will help you place the "givens," or starter numbers, generated by the Bible trivia questions.

2. For each puzzle, trivia questions will be answered by the numbers 1 through 9. The coordinates with each question (for example, A1, C9, H3) indicate where you should insert that particular answer into the sudoku grid. If you don't know the answer and want to find out from the Bible, references are provided. Or if you're really eager to get started, the answers are shown, upside down, underneath the puzzle grid.

3. Once you've inserted the givens into the grid, you can solve the sudoku puzzle. The goal of sudoku is to place the numbers 1 through 9 in each row, each column, and each of nine 3 x 3 minigrids (the shaded areas) within the larger puzzle. Numbers can never be duplicated in a row, column, or 3 x 3 grid—so use your skills of deduction to determine what numbers can or can't go into a particular box.

LETTER-BASED PUZZLES

1. Each 9 x 9 grid includes "givens," as with traditional sudoku puzzles. But in this case, the givens are letters. The nine letters in each row, column, and 3 x 3 minigrid will spell out a biblical word or phrase.

2. Each puzzle has a hint with a reference. Though exact words and phrases may differ from one Bible translation to another, by closely examining the letters of the puzzle, the correct wording can be deduced.

3. Letter-based puzzles are solved in the same manner as the number-based sudoku. Instead of using nine different numbers, you will use nine different letters. When solving, make sure that no letter repeats within any row, any column, or any of the nine 3 x 3 mini grids.

Special thanks to our puzzle contributors: Carrie Brown, Ellen Caughey, N. Teri Grottke, Sara Stoker, and Conover Swofford. We hope you enjoy *Fun Bible Sudoku!*

	A	B	C	D	E	F	G	H	I
1		H				T	M	O	
2	A	T					S		
3	O		L	M				H	I
4				T	I	E			
5	E			A		O			H
6	T			S	H	M			L
7			T					I	
8		L	A					M	
9	S		O	E		L	H	A	T

Hint: Row 6

Esau went __ _____ to get himself yet another wife. (Genesis 28:9)

For B2, I3, D6, G7, A9

How many pieces were some of the Lord's prophets sawed into?
(Hebrews 11:37)

For C1, H3, F4, A5, B7, I8

How many vials in Revelation contained plagues?
(Revelation 21:9)

For C2, E5, F7

How many hundred men came with Esau to meet Jacob? (Genesis 32:6)

For D7, H9

How many sons were born to King David in Jerusalem?
(1 Chronicles 3:5–8)

For E1, I7, A8, F9

How many evil spirits, looking like frogs, did John see coming from a
dragon's mouth? (Revelation 16:13)

For E3, G4, D5, F8, I2

How many hundred years did Shem live after having Arphaxad?
(Genesis 11:11)

For F2, C3, B5

How many years was Abdon judge of Israel? (Judges 12:13–14)

For G1, A3, B4, H5

How many Hebrews did Moses see an Egyptian beating up?
(Exodus 2:11)

For H1, D3, I4, B6, G8, C7

In John's vision of heaven, how many wings did each of the four beasts
have? (Revelation 4:8)

	A	B	C	D	E	F	G	H	I
1	■	■	■	□	□	□	■	■	■
2	■	■	■	□	□	□	■	■	■
3	■	■	■	□	□	□	■	■	■
4	□	□	□	■	■	■	□	□	□
5	□	□	□	■	■	■	□	□	□
6	□	□	□	■	■	■	□	□	□
7	■	■	■	□	□	□	■	■	■
8	■	■	■	□	□	□	■	■	■
9	■	■	■	□	□	□	■	■	■

Starter Numbers in Order:

2, 7, 4, 9, 3, 5, 8, 1, 6

For E2, G6, A4
How many golden lampstands are mentioned in Revelation 1:20?

For A2, E1, G3, B5, H9
How many young men refused the king's meat? (Daniel 1:11–12)

For B1, F5, A6, I7
How many verses are in Psalm 100?

For C2, E5, D7, A8
How many coins did the Good Samaritan give the innkeeper? (Luke 10:35)

For C1, I2, D4, A5, B8, F9
In the ten plagues visited on Egypt, what number plague was locusts?
(Exodus 7:14–10:4)

For B3, H7
How many friends initially came to comfort Job? (Job 2:11)

For H2, I4, F6, B7
How many fingers on each hand did the man of stature in 2 Samuel 21:20
have?

For I1, B4, H5, D6, C9
How many sheep did the shepherd lose in Matthew 18:10–14?

For F1, E4, H8
How many sons did Shem and Aram have? (1 Chronicles 1:17)

A B C D E F G H I

1
2
3
4
5
6
7
8
9

Starter Numbers in Order:
7, 4, 5, 2, 8, 3, 6, 1, 9

For D8, G7, B2

How many sons did Perez have? (1 Chronicles 2:5)

For E7, A4, H6, B9

On which day of creation did God call the gathered waters "Seas"?
(Genesis 1:10–13)

For D6, C4

According to Proverbs, how many things can the earth not bear?
(Proverbs 30:21)

For A8, D1, H9, C5

In the city called "The LORD is there," how many gates were named for Gad?
(Ezekiel 48:34–35)

For G1, D3, F4, B5

How many sons did Leah have? (Genesis 30:20)

For H8, E5, A6, G2, C7

How many years was Aeneas in bed with palsy? (Acts 9:33)

For F6, D2, G9, E8, C1

How many hundred years did Shem live after he had Arphaxad?
(Genesis 11:11)

For A5, I7, H1

How many sons did Abihail have? (1 Chronicles 5:13–14)

For E4, F1

How many cubits long was Og's bed? (Deuteronomy 3:11)

	A	B	C	D	E	F	G	H	I
1	■	■	■	□	□	□	■	■	■
2	■	■	■	□	□	□	■	■	■
3	■	■	■	□	□	□	■	■	■
4	□	□	□	■	■	■	□	□	□
5	□	□	□	■	■	■	□	□	□
6	□	□	□	■	■	■	□	□	□
7	■	■	■	□	□	□	■	■	■
8	■	■	■	□	□	□	■	■	■
9	■	■	■	□	□	□	■	■	■

Starter Numbers in Order:
2, 3, 4, 1, 6, 8, 5, 7, 9

For G8, A7, E1, H6, C5
How many generations did Job live to see? (Job 42:16)

For E7, H8, A3, G1
When Israel's enemies come up against them, in how many ways will they flee? (Deuteronomy 28:7)

For A8, G2, H4, C3
". . .than of the ninety and _____ which went not astray." (Matthew 18:13)

For D2, H5, F8, C7
How many years old was the she goat used in Abraham's covenant with God? (Genesis 15:9)

For F7, C2, B6
How many hundred men followed David before he was king? (1 Samuel 23:13)

For G7, E6, B1, F3, C9
How many hundred years did Adam live after he had Seth? (Genesis 5:4)

For D7, A1, B4
How many tables were to be placed on the right side of the temple? (2 Chronicles 4:8)

For F1, G5, D4
How many years did Elah reign in Israel? (1 Kings 16:8)

For G6, D5, A4, H7
In the city called "The LORD is there," how many gates were named for Asher? (Ezekiel 48:34)

	A	B	C	D	E	F	G	H	I
1	▓	▓	▓				▓	▓	▓
2	▓	▓	▓				▓	▓	▓
3	▓	▓	▓				▓	▓	▓
4				▓	▓	▓			
5				▓	▓	▓			
6				▓	▓	▓			
7	▓	▓	▓				▓	▓	▓
8	▓	▓	▓				▓	▓	▓
9	▓	▓	▓				▓	▓	▓

Starter Numbers in Order:
4, 7, 9, 3, 6, 8, 5, 2, 1

For A5, H8
How many years did Paul stay in his own rented house in Rome?
(Acts 28:30)

For B1, C6, F7
How many measures of barley will sell for a penny during the tribulation?
(Revelation 6:6)

For C1, F3, A4, E7
How many of the tabernacle curtains were to be coupled together?
(Exodus 26:3)

For C3, I4, A6, B7, D8, G9
What was the approximate height in feet of Goliath? (1 Samuel 17:4)

For D1, C2, G3, F5, I7, A8
How many days after Jesus said, "There be some of them that stand here, which shall not taste of death, till they have seen the kingdom of God come with power," did Peter, James, and John see Jesus transfigured on a mountain? (Mark 9:1–2)

For D2, I3, F4, H6, E8, C9
On what day were male babies—descendants of Abraham—to be circumcised? (Genesis 17:12)

For E3, G4, H7, B9
How many heads does the beast of Revelation have? (Revelation 17:7)

For F1, A3, G5, D7, I9
According to Joseph's plan, after paying Egypt's tax, how many fifths of the harvest were left for the people? (Genesis 47:24)

For G2, C4, H5
How many tenths of an ephah is an omer? (Exodus 16:36)

	A	B	C	D	E	F	G	H	I
1	▦	▦	▦				▦	▦	▦
2	▦	▦	▦				▦	▦	▦
3	▦	▦	▦				▦	▦	▦
4				▦	▦	▦			
5				▦	▦	▦			
6				▦	▦	▦			
7	▦	▦	▦				▦	▦	▦
8	▦	▦	▦				▦	▦	▦
9	▦	▦	▦				▦	▦	▦

Starter Numbers in Order:
2, 3, 5, 9, 6, 8, 7, 4, 1

For A3, E6, G1, B4

How were the disciples sent out? (Mark 6:7)

For G6, F4

How many hundred did Adino slay at one time? (2 Samuel 23:8)

For H3, E2, A1, I7, F6

How many days per week was Israel allowed to work? (Exodus 20:9)

For F8, A5, B7

How many thousand proverbs did Solomon speak? (1 Kings 4:32)

For H2, C6, F5, E7

In the list of the Ten Commandments, what number commandment says, "Thou shalt not commit adultery?" (Exodus 20:14)

For H7, D5, F3, B6, G4, E8

Besides the first four, how many other sons did David have with Bathsheba? (1 Chronicles 3:8)

For D8, H4, B9, F1, I2

How many dressed sheep did Abigail take to David? (1 Samuel 25:18)

For C8, H9, E1, G2

In a vision of Daniel, how many heads were on the beast like a leopard? (Daniel 7:6)

For A2, D4

How many kings of Aphek did Joshua smite? (Joshua 12:7, 18)

	A	B	C	D	E	F	G	H	I
1	■	■	■				■	■	■
2	■	■	■				■	■	■
3	■	■	■				■	■	■
4				■	■	■			
5				■	■	■			
6				■	■	■			
7	■	■	■				■	■	■
8	■	■	■				■	■	■
9	■	■	■				■	■	■

Starter Numbers in Order:

2, 8, 6, 3, 7, 9, 5, 4, 1

For D7, B5

How many daughters did Reuel have? (Exodus 2:16)

For H4, A9, C5

What chapter of Romans contains in verse 28 the assurance that God works everything together for our good?

For E1, I4, B6, C3, F9

How many sons did Ham have? (1 Chronicles 1:8)

For A1, I2

Which of the first nine chapters of Acts deals with Anaias and Sapphira?

For D8, H7, C4, E2, A3, G6

How many coins were lost in Luke 15:8–10?

For G3, E9, F4, B2

How many months was Jehoiachin king of Judah? (2 Kings 24:8)

For D6, F3, E7, B4, C2

In the list of the sons of Jesse in 1 Chronicles 2:13–15, what number son is Ozem?

For G1, E6, D9, C8, A4

How many sons did Naomi have? (Ruth 1:2)

For H2, B8, E3, C1, I5

How many Beatitudes are listed in Matthew 5:3–11?

	A	B	C	D	E	F	G	H	I
1	■	■	■				■	■	■
2	■	■	■				■	■	■
3	■	■	■				■	■	■
4				■	■	■			
5				■	■	■			
6				■	■	■			
7	■	■	■				■	■	■
8	■	■	■				■	■	■
9	■	■	■				■	■	■

Starter Numbers in Order:
7, 8, 4, 5, 1, 3, 6, 2, 9

9

For H1, D5, I4, E8

How many sons of Anak did Caleb defeat? (Joshua 15:14)

For C1, F4, E3

In David's confrontation with Nabal, how many hundred "abode by the stuff"? (1 Samuel 25:13)

For G4, E9

According to Eliphaz, how many troubles would God deliver Job from? (Job 5:19)

For H3, E1, I8, G5

How many chamberlains did King Ahasuerus have? (Esther 1:10)

For A6, D7, I1, B9

How many principal men were raised up? (Micah 5:5)

For B6, A8

"Be baptized every ____ of you in the name of Jesus Christ for the remission of sins." (Acts 2:38)

For H8, E6, C7, G2, D1

How many hundred thousand fighting men were numbered in Judah? (2 Samuel 24:9)

For A7, I6, H2

". . .three thousand ____ hundred and thirty." (Nehemiah 7:38)

For F3, B5, D4, A2

How many thousand stalls did Solomon have? (2 Chronicles 9:25)

	A	B	C	D	E	F	G	H	I
1	■	■	■	□	□	□	■	■	■
2	■	■	■	□	□	□	■	■	■
3	■	■	■	□	□	□	■	■	■
4	□	□	□	■	■	■	□	□	□
5	□	□	□	■	■	■	□	□	□
6	□	□	□	■	■	■	□	□	□
7	■	■	■	□	□	□	■	■	■
8	■	■	■	□	□	□	■	■	■
9	■	■	■	□	□	□	■	■	■

Starter Numbers in Order:

3, 2, 6, 7, 8, 1, 5, 9, 4

10

	A	B	C	D	E	F	G	H	I
1	H		I		O		E		
2		M			E		Y	K	
3		Y	N		K		I		O
4				M					
5			O		N	H		L	
6	M	E			L	O	K		N
7	Y						L		M
8	N	L			I				K
9		H	K		M	Y		O	E

Hint: Column F

God promised the Israelite slaves a land flowing with _____ and _____.
(Exodus 3:8)

11

	A	B	C	D	E	F	G	H	I
1	G		S			N	R		O
2	K	I				A		N	
3	F			K	R				
4		K	F	N	S		O	G	
5	R	N				I	F		
6					K			R	A
7				R			A	F	
8	S				N		G		R
9	O		A		G	F		I	

Hint: Column E

What the wayward Israelites confessed doing to the Lord: _____ Him.
(Judges 10:10)

For D9, I3, A7, H6, B4

"Lo, ____ born in my house is mine heir." (Genesis 15:3)

For F4, C2, B9

How many hundred shekels did Abraham pay for the burial cave?
(Genesis 23:16)

For B8, G1, F7

On which day of creation did dry land appear?
(Genesis 1:9–13)

For A3, F1, C5

How many of his officers did Pharaoh put in prison? (Genesis 40:2–3)

For H7, D4, G2

Which verse of Psalm 19 says, "The law of the LORD is perfect, converting
the soul"?

For E1, A9

How many thousand camels did Job have in his latter life?
(Job 42:12)

For E3, I2, A4, F6, C8

"Give a portion to seven, and also to ____." (Ecclesiastes 11:2)

For F2, B3, H5, E4

Hezekiah "reigned _____ and twenty years in Jerusalem."
(2 Chronicles 29:1)

For A8, D2, G7, B5

How many trees were the Amorite kings of Joshua's time hanged on?
(Joshua 10:26)

	A	B	C	D	E	F	G	H	I
1	■	■	■				■	■	■
2	■	■	■				■	■	■
3	■	■	■				■	■	■
4				■	■	■			
5				■	■	■			
6				■	■	■			
7	■	■	■				■	■	■
8	■	■	■				■	■	■
9	■	■	■				■	■	■

Starter Numbers in Order:
1, 4, 3, 2, 7, 6, 8, 9, 5

13

For A1, E3, C4, G5, B9

What number commandment says, "Thou shalt not steal"? (Exodus 20:15)

For C1, I2, A6, G9

How many pillars were made for the tabernacle entrance posts? (Exodus 36:38)

For D1, B3, A4, I5, F8

How many lambs did God tell Ezekiel the prince should sacrifice on the day of the new moon? (Ezekiel 46:6)

For D2, E9

How many times was Paul beaten with rods? (2 Corinthians 11:25)

For D3, A8, F9

How many years did Hoshea reign in Samaria? (2 Kings 17:1)

For G1, E2, C3, H6, I7

In the book of Exodus, how many sheep was a convicted sheep thief to pay in restitution? (Exodus 22:1)

For G3, I4, D5, H8, C9

In Revelation, with how many kings is the beast associated? (Revelation 17:10–11)

For H1, D6, B7, E8

How did Moses describe "the LORD our God"? (Deuteronomy 6:4)

For H4, C6, A7, G8, D9

How many hours did the unruly Ephesian crowd shout its support for the goddess Diana (or Artemis)? (Acts 19:34)

	A	B	C	D	E	F	G	H	I
1	▓	▓	▓				▓	▓	▓
2	▓	▓	▓				▓	▓	▓
3	▓	▓	▓				▓	▓	▓
4				▓	▓	▓			
5				▓	▓	▓			
6				▓	▓	▓			
7	▓	▓	▓				▓	▓	▓
8	▓	▓	▓				▓	▓	▓
9	▓	▓	▓				▓	▓	▓

Starter Numbers in Order:
8, 5, 6, 3, 9, 4, 7, 1, 2

For I3, G5, C7, B4, A2

How many tables were to be placed on the left side of the temple?
(2 Chronicles 4:8)

For E5, I6, A4, F2, B3

How many "were born to the giant in Gath, and fell by the hand of David"?
(2 Samuel 21:22)

For E2, A9, G4, B1

How many men were thrown into the fiery furnace? (Daniel 3:20)

For G1, A5, F6, E8

In the list of foundation stones in Revelation 21:19–20,
what number is topaz?

For B6, D7, I2, C8, F1

How many days did Samson give his wedding guests to solve a riddle?
(Judges 14:12)

For H7, E3

In the city called "The LORD is there," how many gates were named for
Zebulun? (Ezekiel 48:33)

For H8, C5, D6

How many Hebrew midwives were there in the time of Moses?
(Exodus 1:15)

For A1, H6

How many tables did Israel slay the sacrifices on? (Ezekiel 40:41)

For C1, B7, D4

During the fall of Jericho, for how many days did Joshua's armed men march
once around the city? (Joshua 6:3)

	A	B	C	D	E	F	G	H	I
1	▓	▓	▓				▓	▓	▓
2	▓	▓	▓				▓	▓	▓
3	▓	▓	▓				▓	▓	▓
4				▓	▓	▓			
5				▓	▓	▓			
6				▓	▓	▓			
7	▓	▓	▓				▓	▓	▓
8	▓	▓	▓				▓	▓	▓
9	▓	▓	▓				▓	▓	▓

Starter Numbers in Order:
5, 4, 3, 9, 7, 1, 2, 8, 6

15

For D6, G8, B2, C5
How many women bore Jacob's children? (Genesis 35:23–26)

For H4, A6, G9
How many of Moses' siblings are mentioned in Numbers 12:1?

For E6, H9, G1, A7
How many churches are mentioned in Revelation 1:20?

For D2, A3, E9, B4
During the Feast of Tabernacles, how many bullocks were to be prepared for an offering on the fifth day? (Numbers 29:26)

For F6, C9, B1, H2, E8, A5
How many pounds did the man in Luke 19:18 earn for his lord?

For F9, C8, E3
How many verses are in Psalm 23?

For B6, D9, C3, I2
How many things were originally kept in the ark of the covenant? (Hebrews 9:4)

For H6, B9, C2
How many books are mentioned in Revelation 5:1?

For G5, H1, E4, D7
Of the first nine chapters of Proverbs, which chapter begins, "Doth not wisdom cry"?

	A	B	C	D	E	F	G	H	I
1									
2									
3									
4									
5									
6									
7									
8									
9									

Starter Numbers in Order:

4, 2, 7, 9, 5, 6, 3, 1, 8

16

For I3, B8, E4
How many prophets crossed the Jordan River on dry ground before Elijah was taken to heaven? (2 Kings 2:8)

For B4, D1, I5, C2, E7
In the list of the Gadites who joined David, what number was Eliel? (1 Chronicles 12:11)

For F8, A1
How many months was Esther beautified with oil of myrrh? (Esther 2:12)

For G9, B7, C5
How many talents were given to the first man in this parable of Jesus? (Matthew 25:15)

For G7, F5, D9, C1, A8
How many days was Lazarus in the grave? (John 11:17)

For A6, H1, E5
How many sons did Esau have with his wife Adah? (Genesis 36:4)

For H6, C3, E2
Which seal's opening in the book of Revelation resulted in someone being given balances? (Revelation 6:5)

For E9, A5, I2, D4
How many years did Abdon judge Israel? (Judges 12:13–14)

For C7, A4, G8, B2, E1
". . .more than over ninety and ___ just persons." (Luke 15:7)

	A	B	C	D	E	F	G	H	I
1	▒	▒	▒				▒	▒	▒
2	▒	▒	▒				▒	▒	▒
3	▒	▒	▒				▒	▒	▒
4				▒	▒	▒			
5				▒	▒	▒			
6				▒	▒	▒			
7	▒	▒	▒				▒	▒	▒
8	▒	▒	▒				▒	▒	▒
9	▒	▒	▒				▒	▒	▒

Starter Numbers in Order:
2, 7, 6, 5, 4, 1, 3, 8, 9

For A1, D3, H4, E6, B7
How many Midianite kings did the Israelites, under Moses, kill?
(Numbers 31:8)

For B3, F7, G8, C9
How many heads did the huge red dragon of Revelation have?
(Revelation 12:3)

For C3, A4, B8
On which day of creation did God make people? (Genesis 1:27–31)

For F1, B4, I6
On which day of creation did God make the sun and moon?
(Genesis 1:16–19)

For D1, B2, G6, F9
How many days old was the Christ child when he was named "Jesus"?
(Luke 2:21)

For G2, E3, B5, D7
What number plus three was the age of Jesus when He stayed behind in Jerusalem instead of joining Mary and Joseph for the journey home?
(Luke 2:42)

For H1, I5, D6
When Tabitha (or Dorcas) died, how many men were sent to get Peter in the nearby town? (Acts 9:36–38)

For H3, F5, C6, A7, I8, E9
How many nights did God warn Abimelech in a dream about Abraham's wife, Sarah? (Genesis 20:3)

For I1, F3, D4, E7, H9
What number was part of the name of the inns or taverns that Paul saw on his trip to Rome? (Acts 28:15)

A B C D E F G H I

1 2 3 4 5 6 7 8 9

Starter Numbers in Order:
5, 7, 6, 4, 8, 9, 2, 1, 3

For I7, B3, E8, C5, F1

How many curtains were to be coupled together in Exodus 26:3?

For D8, B4, H6, C2

After how many days did Jesus take Peter, James, and John up on a mountain by themselves? (Matthew 17:1)

For F8, I2, H5, C4

How many years was Jehoram king of Judah? (2 Kings 8:16-17)

For F5, C3, I6, B7, D2

Which hour, besides the sixth, is mentioned in Matthew 20:5?

For G1, A6, E7, H8

How many brothers of Goliath are listed in 2 Samuel 21:19?

For H3, F2, D9, A1

How many seals were on the book in John's vision of heaven? (Revelation 5:1)

For G4, H7, D5, B1

What was the breadth in cubits of the tabernacle curtains? (Exodus 26:8)

For G2, E3, H4, D6

How many thieves were crucified with Jesus? (Matthew 27:38)

For E1, I4, B5

How many sons did Noah begat? (Genesis 5:32)

Starter Numbers in Order:
5, 6, 8, 9, 1, 7, 4, 2, 3

For I3, A4

"Let us not therefore judge ___ another any more." (Romans 14:13)

For I6, D3, A5, B9, C2

How many chapters are in the book of Habakkuk?

For E1, G5, D8

Of the lots cast for temple duty, what number lot fell to Mattaniah?
(1 Chronicles 25:16)

For F7, I4, B5, H8, C3, G2, D1

How many hundred years did Lamech live after he had Noah?
(Genesis 5:30)

For C1, F3, H4, E9

How many measures of barley did Boaz give Ruth? (Ruth 3:15)

For B7, H1, G4

In John 1:35-37, how many disciples of John the Baptist went and
followed Jesus?

For D2, A7

How many faces did each of the living creatures have? (Ezekiel 1:5-6)

For B1, E2, C5

How many days old was a man child to be when he was circumcised?
(Genesis 17:12)

For D4, F9, C7

Which verse of Philippians 4 says that the peace of God passes all
understanding?

	A	B	C	D	E	F	G	H	I
1	▓	▓	▓				▓	▓	▓
2	▓	▓	▓				▓	▓	▓
3	▓	▓	▓				▓	▓	▓
4				▓	▓	▓			
5				▓	▓	▓			
6				▓	▓	▓			
7	▓	▓	▓				▓	▓	▓
8	▓	▓	▓				▓	▓	▓
9	▓	▓	▓				▓	▓	▓

Starter Numbers in Order:
1, 3, 9, 5, 6, 2, 4, 8, 7

20

	A	B	C	D	E	F	G	H	I
1		S			G		R	A	
2	D		R	P					E
3	G			I				D	
4	A	R	I	S		P	G		
5					A	R			D
6			E		I	G	A	S	
7			G	R				O	A
8		A	O		E			I	
9		P				S	E	R	

Hint: Column C

We should continually offer the sacrifice of _____ to ___.
(Hebrews 13:15)

21

	A	B	C	D	E	F	G	H	I
1		T	I	O		G			Y
2	O				E			T	
3	Y		M	I					N
4	G			E		Y			
5		Y		N	M	O	T		G
6			O	H		T		N	
7		M			Y	I			
8			G			E	N		M
9	T	H		M	O			G	I

Hint: Column G

A title for Jesus: _____ ___ of Jacob. (Isaiah 60:16)

For C1, F8, H5, D4

How many princes of the Midianites did Gideon's army slay? (Judges 7:25)

For G5, B4, D3

Of the oxen holding up the molten sea at Solomon's temple, how many faced in each direction? (2 Chronicles 4:4)

For B6, E3, H8, D9

How many times was the blood sprinkled before the Lord? (Leviticus 4:6)

For F7, C5

". . .every ___ after his tongue. . ." (Genesis 10:5)

For F4, A8, D1, G9

". . .___ hundred and fifty and six." (1 Chronicles 9:9)

For I4, B3, H2, F6

How many paces did the ark go before the sacrifice was made?
(2 Samuel 6:13)

For E9, A3, I6, C4

How many hundred pomegranates were on the two wreaths on the temple's pillars? (2 Chronicles 4:13)

For B2, I5, C7, G1

How many hundred years old was Noah when he had his children?
(Genesis 5:32)

For G3, E5, F2, B7

In the first nine psalms, which psalm begins, "O LORD, our Lord, how excellent is thy name in all the earth!"?

	A	B	C	D	E	F	G	H	I
1	▓	▓	▓				▓	▓	▓
2	▓	▓	▓				▓	▓	▓
3	▓	▓	▓				▓	▓	▓
4				▓	▓	▓			
5				▓	▓	▓			
6				▓	▓	▓			
7	▓	▓	▓				▓	▓	▓
8	▓	▓	▓				▓	▓	▓
9	▓	▓	▓				▓	▓	▓

Starter Numbers in Order:
2, 3, 7, 1, 9, 6, 4, 5, 8

For A1, E3, D6, C7

How many years could one have a Hebrew slave serve them?
(Jeremiah 34:14)

For B1, D4, H7, E9

How many languages did the world's people speak when they started building the tower of Babel? (Genesis 11:1-9)

For D3, A6, G9

How many sons did Jesse have? (1 Samuel 17:12)

For E1, I5

How many thousand people were killed in Revelation's earthquake in Jerusalem? (Revelation 11:13)

For F1, A2, I3, G7

How many thousand men did Joshua use to ambush enemies near Ai?
(Joshua 8:10-12)

For G1, C2, I4, E7, A8

What number in the list of the fruit of the Spirit is joy? (Galatians 5:22-23)

For G2, A4, E5, H6, F7, C9

In Jesus' parable, how many years had a fig tree produced no fruit before its owner threatened to cut it down? (Luke 13:7)

For H1, E4, G5, C6, B8

How many months (plus twenty days) did it take Joab to make a census of Israel and Judah? (2 Samuel 24:2, 8)

For I1, C3, B4, D7, H8, A9

How many rows of stones were on the breastplate of judgment?
(Exodus 28:15-17)

	A	B	C	D	E	F	G	H	I
1	░	░	░				░	░	░
2	░	░	░				░	░	░
3	░	░	░				░	░	░
4				░	░	░			
5				░	░	░			
6				░	░	░			
7	░	░	░				░	░	░
8	░	░	░				░	░	░
9	░	░	░				░	░	░

Starter Numbers in Order:

6, 1, 8, 7, 5, 2, 3, 9, 4

For D9, B7, G5, C3
How many years was Joash hidden in the house of God?
(2 Chronicles 22:11–12)

For I7, F6, C8, H1, D2
How many living creatures are described in Ezekiel 1:5?

For A8, F2, H4, D5
How many trumpets are mentioned in Revelation 8:2?

For F3, B1, H9, E4
How many loaves did Jesus miraculously multiply into a dinner for five thousand people? (Matthew 14:17)

For C5, G7, D1, F8
How many bullocks are mentioned in Numbers 29:26?

For I3, B2, E8
How many soldiers pierced Jesus' side with a spear? (John 19:34)

For E3, C2, B5, F7
In Matthew 23:13, how many groups did Jesus pronounce woes upon?

For A3, I6, D7, G1
How many wives did Esau have? (Genesis 36:2–3)

For G6, C4, E5
How many oxen did Moses give to the sons of Merari? (Numbers 7:8)

	A	B	C	D	E	F	G	H	I
1	▓	▓	▓				▓	▓	▓
2	▓	▓	▓				▓	▓	▓
3	▓	▓	▓				▓	▓	▓
4				▓	▓	▓			
5				▓	▓	▓			
6				▓	▓	▓			
7	▓	▓	▓				▓	▓	▓
8	▓	▓	▓				▓	▓	▓
9	▓	▓	▓				▓	▓	▓

Starter Numbers in Order:

6, 4, 7, 5, 9, 1, 2, 3, 8

For F7, G6, A2, E4

How many sons did Leah have? (Genesis 30:20)

For I7, H5, B4

How many chapters are in the book of Jude?

For G5, C1, D2, B9

How many men carried the paralytic to Jesus to be cured? (Mark 2:3)

For F2, H1, C6

How many wives did Jacob have? (Genesis 29:23–28)

For G8, E9, F4, B3

How many crosses were on the hill of Golgotha? (Mark 15:27)

For D4, A1, H3, C8

How many years did Jacob agree to serve in order to get Rachel as his wife? (Genesis 29:18)

For C4, B1, D8, H2

Of the first nine verses in 1 Chronicles 3, which one mentions David's daughter?

For H8, E7, B5, D6, C3

How many pillars were made for the hanging in the tabernacle? (Exodus 26:37)

For F5, D7, H4, E3

What number times five equals the days and nights Jesus fasted before meeting Satan? (Matthew 4:1–2)

	A	B	C	D	E	F	G	H	I
1									
2									
3									
4									
5									
6									
7									
8									
9									

Starter Numbers in Order:
6, 1, 4, 2, 3, 7, 9, 5, 8

For F3, B6, G9, C1, E8
What number commandment says, "Remember the sabbath day to keep it holy"? (Exodus 20:8)

For A8, D7, E3, C6
While witnessing the Transfiguration, how many tabernacles did Peter want to build? (Matthew 17:4)

For I3, C2, D6
How many mites did the widow put into the treasury? (Luke 21:2)

For H7, F1, I4
How many verses are in Psalm 150?

For G7, B1, F4, C8
How many kings of Shimron-meron did Joshua smite? (Joshua 12:7, 20)

For C9, G5, D2
How many maidens were given to Esther? (Esther 2:9)

For D4, G1, A5, F9, B8, E2
How many people were on the ark? (Genesis 7:13)

For B5, I6, A2
In the list of the Gadites who joined David, what number was Elzabad? (1 Chronicles 12:8, 12)

For I1, B7, D9
In what year of King Rehoboam's reign did King Shishak of Egypt attack and take treasures of the temple? (1Kings 14:25–26)

	A	B	C	D	E	F	G	H	I
1	■	■	■	□	□	□	■	■	■
2	■	■	■	□	□	□	■	■	■
3	■	■	■	□	□	□	■	■	■
4	□	□	□	■	■	■	□	□	□
5	□	□	□	■	■	■	□	□	□
6	□	□	□	■	■	■	□	□	□
7	■	■	■	□	□	□	■	■	■
8	■	■	■	□	□	□	■	■	■
9	■	■	■	□	□	□	■	■	■

Starter Numbers in Order:
4, 3, 2, 6, 1, 7, 8, 9, 5

For H9, B4, G6, E5

On what day of creation did plant life appear? (Genesis 1:11–13)

For B1, G2, C6, F9

How many horns were on the altar? (Exodus 27:1–2)

For H4, D7

How many kings are mentioned in Genesis 14:2?

For F1, I2, A3, G7, B5, D4

In the city called "The LORD is there," how many gates were named for Naphtali? (Ezekiel 48:34–35)

For B9, F3, C1

In Revelation 15:6, how many angels had plagues?

For I4, C9, F7, G1, E6

Peleg lived two hundred and _____ years after he begat Reu. (Genesis 11:19)

For D5, A9, E2, C3

Which seal's opening in heaven resulted in someone being given a sword? (Revelation 6:3–4)

For C4, E8, B2

How many days are mentioned in John 20:26?

For H1, G5, I8

In the foundation stones listed in Revelation 21:19–20, what number is sardius (carnelian, NIV)?

	A	B	C	D	E	F	G	H	I
1	▨	▨	▨				▨	▨	▨
2	▨	▨	▨				▨	▨	▨
3	▨	▨	▨				▨	▨	▨
4				▨	▨	▨			
5				▨	▨	▨			
6				▨	▨	▨			
7	▨	▨	▨				▨	▨	▨
8	▨	▨	▨				▨	▨	▨
9	▨	▨	▨				▨	▨	▨

Starter Numbers in Order:

3, 4, 5, 1, 7, 9, 2, 8, 6

For A9

How many chief men of their fathers' houses were among the sons of Ithamar? (1 Chronicles 24:4)

For H4, D5, G9

How many year-old lambs without spot were to be presented as a daily offering, per Old Testament law? (Numbers 28:3)

For E4, G3, B1

In what year of the captivity of King Jehoiachin did Ezekiel begin prophesying? (Ezekiel 1:2–3)

For B7, A6, G2

The branches represented how many days? (Genesis 40:12)

For F7, B5, E3, D4, C1

How many times hotter was Nebuchadnezzar's furnace heated for Shadrach, Meshach, and Abednego? (Daniel 3:19)

For H7, C8, D6, E1

How many years did a Hebrew slave have to serve before he could be set free? (Deuteronomy 15:12)

For A5, E2, I1, D9, G4

According to Isaiah 5:10, ten acres of vineyards yielded how many baths of wine?

For E8, B4, H6, C9

How many corners of the earth is Judah dispersed to? (Isaiah 11:12)

For F2, A3, G7, B9

At what hour did Jesus say from the cross, "Why hast thou forsaken me?" (Matthew 27:46)

	A	B	C	D	E	F	G	H	I
1									
2									
3									
4									
5									
6									
7									
8									
9									

Starter Numbers in Order:
8, 2, 5, 3, 7, 6, 1, 4, 9

	A	B	C	D	E	F	G	H	I
1	H			B				E	A
2		B	E			A	F		H
3	A	D			H				
4	F				B	E			R
5		I		D	S			A	
6	D			F	R			S	B
7					D			H	
8	E		B	S			I		D
9	I	A				R			S

Hint: Column D

Jesus multiplied _____ and _____ in His miracle. (Matthew 14:19)

	A	B	C	D	E	F	G	H	I
1	T	R		S			I	B	
2	I			R			H	O	
3	B		N	E		I		R	
4	S				R			N	
5	O	E		B			T	I	
6	H				T		E		
7		I	S		E	H		T	B
8			O			R			
9	R	H		N			O		S

Hint: Column H

Line of lyrics from a popular Christmas hymn, Noel: ____ __ ___ King of Israel. (Matthew 2:2)

For I8, B6, F3, E7

How many kinds of death did the Lord appoint to Judah? (Jeremiah 15:3)

For A6, D1, I5, C2, E4

On what day did Abidan present an offering? (Numbers 7:60)

For F1, I2, A7, D8, H4

How many talents were given to the third man in a parable of Jesus? (Matthew 25:14–15)

For G8, C7, B4, E9, I1

How many hundred chosen chariots did Pharaoh send after Israel? (Exodus 14:7)

For G5, B9

How many hundred of Gideon's men lapped the water? (Judges 7:7)

For A4, H8

According to an angel in Revelation, how many kings are fallen? (Revelation 17:10)

For E1, G7, C3

How many years did Israel serve Chushan-rishathaim? (Judges 3:8)

For H1, A2, D7

How many sons did Eli have? (1 Samuel 1:3)

For H3, C4

How old was Jehoash when he began to reign? (2 Kings 11:21)

	A	B	C	D	E	F	G	H	I
1	▓	▓	▓				▓	▓	▓
2	▓	▓	▓				▓	▓	▓
3	▓	▓	▓				▓	▓	▓
4				▓	▓	▓			
5				▓	▓	▓			
6				▓	▓	▓			
7	▓	▓	▓				▓	▓	▓
8	▓	▓	▓				▓	▓	▓
9	▓	▓	▓				▓	▓	▓

Starter Numbers in Order:
7 ,2 ,8 ,5 ,3 ,6 ,1 ,9 ,4

For C1, E5, H9

How many escaped Lot's kidnappers to report to Abram what had happened? (Genesis 14:12–13)

For D1, A2, F4, E7, B8

How many Amorite kings joined forces to attack the city of Gibeon? (Joshua 10:5)

For E2, H3, G5, D6

In Revelation, how many thunders did the voice of an angel sound like? (Revelation 10:1, 3)

For F1, B2, I4, D5, H8

How many days had a multitude been with Jesus before He fed them? (Mark 8:2)

For F3, A5, G7

What number results from subtracting the number of horsemen in Revelation from the number of Jesus' disciples? (Revelation 6:1–8; Matthew 10:1)

For G1, A4, E6, F9, C8

How many wagons or carts were given to the Merari Levites for their service with the tabernacle? (Numbers 7:8)

For G2, C3, B5, I9

What number plus 3 equals the number of Jesus' apostles? (Matthew 10:2)

For H1, E3, I8, A9

How many possible replacements for Judas Iscariot did the eleven apostles test by lot? (Acts 1:23–25)

For I1, H5, C6, B7, D9

In Isaiah's vision, how many wings did each seraphim have? (Isaiah 6:2)

	A	B	C	D	E	F	G	H	I
1	■	■	■	□	□	□	■	■	■
2	■	■	■	□	□	□	■	■	■
3	■	■	■	□	□	□	■	■	■
4	□	□	□	■	■	■	□	□	□
5	□	□	□	■	■	■	□	□	□
6	□	□	□	■	■	■	□	□	□
7	■	■	■	□	□	□	■	■	■
8	■	■	■	□	□	□	■	■	■
9	■	■	■	□	□	□	■	■	■

Starter Numbers in Order:
1, 5, 7, 3, 8, 4, 9, 2, 6

For I5, C3, F4, E9
In the list of the Gadites who joined David, what number is Attai?
(1 Chronicles 12:8, 11)

For G3, B5, I6, D1
All the days of Methuselah were nine hundred and sixty ____.
(Genesis 5:27)

For B3, F5, C8
How many damsels did Abigail take with her to go to David?
(1 Samuel 25:42)

For H5, A6, C7, F9
How many days was Zimri king of Israel? (1 Kings 16:15)

For E5, B7
How many years was the famine in the time of David? (2 Samuel 21:1)

For I7, C5, F1, E6, H2
How many sons did Kohath have? (1 Chronicles 23:12)

For H1, E7
Which verse of Psalm 23 begins, "The LORD is my shepherd"?

For D6, G7, B9, F3, C2
"Behold, there come ____ woes more hereafter." (Revelation 9:12)

For A8, G2, E3
". . .about an ____ days after these sayings. . ." (Luke 9:28)

	A	B	C	D	E	F	G	H	I
1	▓	▓	▓				▓	▓	▓
2	▓	▓	▓				▓	▓	▓
3	▓	▓	▓				▓	▓	▓
4				▓	▓	▓			
5				▓	▓	▓			
6				▓	▓	▓			
7	▓	▓	▓				▓	▓	▓
8	▓	▓	▓				▓	▓	▓
9	▓	▓	▓				▓	▓	▓

Starter Numbers in Order:
6, 9, 5, 7, 3, 4, 1, 2, 8

For G4, H1, E2, C6
How many debtors are mentioned in Luke 7:41?

For I5, D4, H7, G2
Of the first nine psalms, which one begins, "Blessed is the man that walketh not in the counsel of the ungodly"?

For A7, F1, E5
How many days were the men of war to march once around the city of Jericho? (Joshua 6:3)

For E4, D7, I2, C1
How many cubits was the wing of one cherub in the most holy house in Solomon's temple? (2 Chronicles 3:10–11)

For D6, F9, B4, E1, C3
How many chapters are in the book of Jonah?

For C4, H5, A1, E8, B7
According to 1 Samuel 17:12, how many sons did Jesse have?

For D8, C5, B3
How many stars are mentioned in Revelation 1:20?

For G3, B2, H9, C8
How many sons did David's sister Zeruiah have? (1 Chronicles 2:16)

For G1
What number times 100 was the number of iron chariots belonging to Sisera? (Judges 4:2–3)

	A	B	C	D	E	F	G	H	I
1									
2									
3									
4									
5									
6									
7									
8									
9									

Starter Numbers in Order:
2, 1, 6, 5, 4, 8, 7, 3, 9

35

For H7, B1, F5, C6

How many daughters did Shimei have? (1 Chronicles 4:27)

For F2, C9, E8

How many hundred thousand were in Jeroboam's army? (2 Chronicles 13:3)

For D7, G1, A4

How many things did David desire of the Lord? (Psalm 27:4)

For F4, C1, D2

How many days and nights was Jonah in the belly of the fish? (Jonah 1:17)

For I1, F8, C4, H6

Of the first nine chapters in Genesis, which one contains in verse 14 the promise of the rainbow?

For A8, I7, B4

How many cubits high was the Egyptian of great stature? (1 Chronicles 11:23)

For B9, I2, A3, D4

According to Genesis 5:7, Seth lived eight hundred and _____ years after he begat Enos.

For E1, A5, G3, C2

How many sons are in the parable of the prodigal son? (Luke 15:11)

For G2, I8, H5

How many wagons did Moses give the sons of Merari? (Numbers 7:8)

	A	B	C	D	E	F	G	H	I
1	░	░	░				░	░	░
2	░	░	░				░	░	░
3	░	░	░				░	░	░
4				░	░	░			
5				░	░	░			
6				░	░	░			
7	░	░	░				░	░	░
8	░	░	░				░	░	░
9	░	░	░				░	░	░

Starter Numbers in Order:
6, 8, 1, 3, 9, 5, 7, 2, 4

For D7, G1, A8

How many hundred chariots did Sisera have? (Judges 4:13)

For C3, H9, B5, D6

According to the book of Jeremiah, how many evils had God's people committed? (Jeremiah 2:13)

For G2, F1

How many sons were born to Ruth and Boaz? (Ruth 4:13)

For C4, E6, A1

How many headwaters came out of Eden? (Genesis 2:10)

For H4, D8, E3

How many kings hid in the cave? (Joshua 10:17)

For I6, C1, D3

In the first nine chapters of Revelation, which chapter contains the sounding of the first of four angels?

For E1, A9, I5, B6

According to John, how many bear witness in earth that Jesus is the Son of God? (1 John 5:8)

For F4, H7, B9

How many names were to be put on one stone? (Exodus 28:10)

For B3, E5, G8, D2

How many loaves of bread did the disciples have in Matthew 15:33–34?

	A	B	C	D	E	F	G	H	I
1	▩	▩	▩				▩	▩	▩
2	▩	▩	▩				▩	▩	▩
3	▩	▩	▩				▩	▩	▩
4				▩	▩	▩			
5				▩	▩	▩			
6				▩	▩	▩			
7	▩	▩	▩				▩	▩	▩
8	▩	▩	▩				▩	▩	▩
9	▩	▩	▩				▩	▩	▩

Starter Numbers in Order:
9, 2, 1, 4, 5, 8, 3, 6, 7

For E6, C1, I3, D9
How many steps did Solomon's throne have? (1 Kings 10:19)

For D3, G7, C4
How old was Mephibosheth when his father Jonathan was killed?
(2 Samuel 4:4)

For B2, G9, E8
How many swords did the disciples have the night of Jesus' arrest?
(Luke 22:38)

For H1, F4, A8, G5
How many thousand men fled before the men of Ai? (Joshua 7:4)

For D7, B4, E2, C3
How many corners of Job's oldest son's house "were smote"?
(Job 1:18–19)

For I2, A6, E7
How many tribes were left to receive their inheritance? (Numbers 34:13)

For H4
How many sons did David's sister Abigail have? (1 Chronicles 2:17)

For G1, C9, F8, I5
How many lamps are mentioned in Exodus 25:37?

For C2, D1, B9
Which verse of Psalm 19 says, "The statutes of the LORD are right"?

	A	B	C	D	E	F	G	H	I
1	■	■	■	□	□	□	■	■	■
2	■	■	■	□	□	□	■	■	■
3	■	■	■	□	□	□	■	■	■
4	□	□	□	■	■	■	□	□	□
5	□	□	□	■	■	■	□	□	□
6	□	□	□	■	■	■	□	□	□
7	■	■	■	□	□	□	■	■	■
8	■	■	■	□	□	□	■	■	■
9	■	■	■	□	□	□	■	■	■

Starter Numbers in Order:
6, 5, 2, 3, 4, 9, 1, 7, 8

	A	B	C	D	E	F	G	H	I
1		O		C	H	I	N	T	A
2	I				R			H	
3				O			C		
4	A	N							H
5	S				O	C		N	
6	C		I	H				S	
7		I	N		C				
8	O			N	I		T		C
9			C	R				I	

Hint: Row 4

__ _____ is considered a very foolish bird in the Bible. (Job 39:13–17)

39

	A	B	C	D	E	F	G	H	I
1		H				W		N	
2			O			G	W	H	T
3	N		G	I					
4	H			W	E			G	
5			T	H	G			I	
6			L					E	W
7	L		I		W		E	T	
8		N	W		I			L	O
9	O			G			N		

Hint: Row 1

___ _____ kine carried the captured ark back to Israel. (1 Samuel 6:12)

For G2, F4, B1, I5
In the list of Jesse's sons in 1 Chronicles 2:13–15, which number son is Raddai?

For H8, D4, F2, G1
How many months was Jehoahaz king of Judah? (2 Kings 23:31)

For A3, E4, H1, B9
How many Gospels are there in the New Testament?

For I3, B8, F9, E1, H5
How many angels came from the east in Revelation 7:2?

For D7, B3, C4, G9
How many daughters-in-law did Naomi have? (Ruth 1:4)

For E5, F1, B7
On what day did God rest? (Genesis 2:3)

For G8, F3, B6, A7
How many chapters are in the book of 1 Timothy?

For C7, E8, H9, D3, G5
How many years was Hoshea king of Israel? (2 Kings 17:1)

For F8, A5, H3, D1
What number times five was the number of years Saul son of Cis ruled Israel? (Acts 13:21)

	A	B	C	D	E	F	G	H	I
1	■	■	■				■	■	■
2	■	■	■				■	■	■
3	■	■	■				■	■	■
4				■	■	■			
5				■	■	■			
6				■	■	■			
7	■	■	■				■	■	■
8	■	■	■				■	■	■
9	■	■	■				■	■	■

Starter Numbers in Order:
5, 3, 4, 1, 2, 7, 6, 9, 8

For H7, A5, I4, F3
How many of Aaron's sons were devoured by fire? (Leviticus 10:1–2)

For G4, B3, I1, C9, D2
How many days was Saul without sight? (Acts 9:9)

For D5, B9, E8, A2, C4
Which verse in Daniel 1 says that Daniel purposed in his heart not to defile himself?

For G6, D3, I7
How many days was Saul supposed to wait for Samuel? (1 Samuel 10:8)

For F4, B2, C6
How many angels are mentioned in Revelation 7:1?

For I5, D6, E3, F9, C2
How many months (plus twenty days) did it take Joab to number the people of Israel and Judah? (2 Samuel 24:1–2, 8)

For H9, F6
How many cubits was the breadth of Nebuchadnezzar's golden image? (Daniel 3:1)

For G1, E7
Which angel's sounding in Revelation resulted in a locust plague? (Revelation 9:1–3)

For D7, A3, I2, C8
How many chapters are in the book of Obadiah?

	A	B	C	D	E	F	G	H	I
1									
2									
3									
4									
5									
6									
7									
8									
9									

Starter Numbers in Order:

2, 3, 8, 7, 4, 9, 6, 5, 1

For A1, I3, F4, C7

In John's Revelation, how many angels stood before God? (Revelation 8:2)

For B2, E4, C5, H7, A8, F9

How many swords did the disciples find on the night of Jesus' arrest? (Luke 22:38)

For B3, D4, I5, E8

According to the prophet Amos, how many months away from harvest did the Lord threaten to withhold rain from idolatrous Israel? (Amos 4:7)

For C1, B4, H5, G8, D9

What kind of "flesh" is there when a man cleaves unto his wife? (Genesis 2:24)

For E2, H4, A6, B7

After Joshua died, how many Philistine rulers did God leave to teach warfare to the Israelites? (Judges 3:2–3)

For F1, C2, H3, A4, E5, B9

After his personal tragedy, how many thousand camels was Job blessed with? (Job 42:12)

For G1, E3, I4, H9

On what day of his young life was John the Baptist circumcised? (Luke 1:59–60)

For G2, C4, H6, I9

How many feet characterized the flying insects the Israelites were forbidden to eat? (Leviticus 11:23)

For G4, E7

How many hundred iron chariots did Sisera have to oppose Deborah's army? (Judges 4:1–4)

	A	B	C	D	E	F	G	H	I
1	▓	▓	▓				▓	▓	▓
2	▓	▓	▓				▓	▓	▓
3	▓	▓	▓				▓	▓	▓
4				▓	▓	▓			
5				▓	▓	▓			
6				▓	▓	▓			
7	▓	▓	▓				▓	▓	▓
8	▓	▓	▓				▓	▓	▓
9	▓	▓	▓				▓	▓	▓

Starter Numbers in Order:

7, 2, 3, 1, 5, 6, 8, 4, 9

For H1, C6, D2

How many ribs did God take out of Adam to make Eve? (Genesis 2:21)

For G9, A8, H4, B5

How many thousand were officers and judges? (1 Chronicles 23:4)

For B2, I1, D7

According to 1 Kings 7:10, the foundation stones for Solomon's palace were ten cubits and some were _____ cubits.

For D8, C3, F1

How many of Adam and Eve's sons are mentioned by name in Genesis 4?

For E7, B4, G5, D1

How many daughters did Philip the evangelist have? (Acts 21:8-9)

For H9, E2, D5, A6

On which day of creation did God divide the waters? (Genesis 1:6-8)

For D9, A4, I2, C8

How many brothers did Joseph present to Pharaoh? (Genesis 47:2)

For A5, H8, G1

According to God's laws given through Moses, which year could the Israelites eat the old fruit? (Leviticus 25:22)

For G2, E4, I7

How many ewe lambs did Abraham give as a witness? (Genesis 21:30)

A B C D E F G H I

1 2 3 4 5 6 7 8 9

Starter Numbers in Order:
1, 6, 8, 3, 4, 2, 5, 9, 7

For D3, I4, A7, F5

In the list of spies in Numbers 13:1–16, what number spy is Shaphat?

For H3, I5, D2

In the list of men in Acts 6:5, what number is Prochorus?

For F9, I2, B4, H5, C8

In the list of priests in Nehemiah 12:1–7, what number priest is Shechaniah?

For I7, C3

In the list of those priests who put their seal on the document in Nehemiah 10:1–8, what number is Nehemiah?

For C2, B9

How many cities are mentioned in Joshua 15:58–59?

For E7, G6, B8

How many words of understanding did Paul say he would rather speak? (1 Corinthians 14:19)

For A5, F4, H1, D9

In the list of David's sons in 1 Chronicles 3:1–9, what number is Shobab?

For D6, F2, A8, I1, C4

At what hour did Jesus say, "*Eli, Eli, lama sabachthani?*" (Matthew 27:46)

For F1, B6, G4, E5

In the list of the sons of Israel in 1 Chronicles 2:1–2, what number is Judah?

	A	B	C	D	E	F	G	H	I
1	░	░	░				░	░	░
2	░	░	░				░	░	░
3	░	░	░				░	░	░
4				░	░	░			
5				░	░	░			
6				░	░	░			
7	░	░	░				░	░	░
8	░	░	░				░	░	░
9	░	░	░				░	░	░

Starter Numbers in Order:
2, 3, 7, 1, 6, 5, 8, 9, 4

45

For A1, H4, B5, F7

How many weeks passed in which Daniel ate no meat, after his vision of a man? (Daniel 10:3–5)

For B2, E3, H5, C6, G8, A9

How many days per year did Israel's daughters lament Jephthah's daughter? (Judges 11:40)

For C3, G5, I7, A8, E9

How many choice sheep were prepared for Governor Nehemiah each day? (Nehemiah 5:18)

For E1, H8, D9

What number times 10 was the age of Sarah when she was told she would bare Isaac? (Genesis 17:15–17)

For E2, I4, C7, G9

How many men did Joseph's ten brothers say fathered them? (Genesis 42:11)

For F2, A5, I6

How old was Josiah when he became king of Judah? (2 Chronicles 34:1)

For G1, C4, I5, D6, E8, H9

How many seals are on the book to be opened by the Lion of the tribe of Judah? (Revelation 5:5)

For G2, D4, C5, E7, B9

When the Son of man is revealed, how many women will be grinding when one is taken? (Luke 17:30, 35)

For I2, E5

How many warriors did the Danites send to spy out the land of Laish? (Judges 18:2)

	A	B	C	D	E	F	G	H	I
1	▓	▓	▓				▓	▓	▓
2	▓	▓	▓				▓	▓	▓
3	▓	▓	▓				▓	▓	▓
4				▓	▓	▓			
5				▓	▓	▓			
6				▓	▓	▓			
7	▓	▓	▓				▓	▓	▓
8	▓	▓	▓				▓	▓	▓
9	▓	▓	▓				▓	▓	▓

Starter Numbers in Order:
3, 4, 6, 9, 1, 8, 7, 2, 5

46

For F8, B5

In a vision of Daniel, how many horns came up from the broken horn on the goat? (Daniel 8:8)

For I1, A7, D4

How many chapters are in the book of 1 Thessalonians?

For E4, G5, A6, F7, B8

How many sons did Uzzi have? (1 Chronicles 7:3)

For F1, G4, B3, C9

According to Jesus' reference to Old Testament law, the testimony of how many men is true? (John 8:17)

For A3, F5, H9, E2

How many men did Ishmael escape with? (Jeremiah 41:15)

For I2, B4, D1

How many hundred years did Enoch walk with God after he begat Methuselah? (Genesis 5:22)

For H3, A1, I6, G7

How many fingers did the giant of Gath have on each hand?
(1 Chronicles 20:6)

For F6, C7, I5, E3

In the first nine chapters of Isaiah, which chapter in verse 6 describes Jesus as "Wonderful"?

For B6

In the list of the ten plagues God visited on Egypt, what number is hail and fire? (Exodus 9:13–35)

	A	B	C	D	E	F	G	H	I
1	■	■	■				■	■	■
2	■	■	■				■	■	■
3	■	■	■				■	■	■
4				■	■	■			
5				■	■	■			
6				■	■	■			
7	■	■	■				■	■	■
8	■	■	■				■	■	■
9	■	■	■				■	■	■

Starter Numbers in Order:
4, 5, 1, 2, 8, 3, 6, 9, 7

For G7, C2, E9, B6, D4
In Pharaoh's dream, how many kine were fatfleshed and well favoured? (Genesis 41:18)

For C6, F5, A3, B9, G2, D7
How many chapters are in the book of Haggai?

For H3, D9, A4
Which verse of Psalm 100 says, "We are his people, and the sheep of his pasture"?

For A1, E7, C8
How many lepers returned to thank Jesus after He cleansed them? (Luke 17:15–17)

For B4, H7, F8
On what day after His birth was Jesus named? (Luke 2:21)

For I5, B2, F3, D8
How many chief porters were at the temple? (1 Chronicles 9:26)

For A2, H6, I1, C5
In what chapter of Luke does Herod admit to having beheaded John the Baptist?

For H2, D5, F7, C1
How many years were the Israelites to sow their land? (Exodus 23:10)

For G1, C9, H4, E8
The altar in Exodus 27:1 was how many cubits long?

	A	B	C	D	E	F	G	H	I
1	■	■	■				■	■	■
2	■	■	■				■	■	■
3	■	■	■				■	■	■
4				■	■	■			
5				■	■	■			
6				■	■	■			
7	■	■	■				■	■	■
8	■	■	■				■	■	■
9	■	■	■				■	■	■

Starter Numbers in Order:
7, 2, 3, 1, 8, 4, 9, 6, 5

	A	B	C	D	E	F	G	H	I
1		S	I	O	T	U		E	R
2			U					T	I
3		O		R				U	
4	I			E		G			H
5		E		U	S		I		
6					H			S	E
7		U	H	S	G		T		
8	S	R					E		
9				H	U		G	R	

Hint: Column I
God saw Noah was this before him: _____. (Genesis 7:1)

49

	A	B	C	D	E	F	G	H	I
1		F	C				A	M	U
2		A	L	C		U			
3	E				A				C
4			F			A	R		
5			E	R				U	L
6	U		I		M			E	
7	L		R	I			E		F
8		U	A		R				I
9	I				L				R

Hint: Row 5

The Lord thy God is _ _____ God. (Deuteronomy 4:31)

For H5, C3, I1, G8
Proverbs 6:16 says that the Lord hates how many things?

For G9, A5, D4
In the list of Gadites who joined David, what number is Johanan?
(1 Chronicles 12:8, 12)

For I8, D1, G4
Song of Solomon 6:9 mentions how many doves?

For H1, B6, F2, C9
How many shekels of silver were given in valuation for a female one month to five years old? (Leviticus 27:6)

For E7, B3, G2, C6
How many kings of the Amorites attacked Gibeon? (Joshua 10:5)

For I6, A2, F4, D7
How many lepers didn't return to thank Jesus? (Luke 17:12–17)

For B9, I3, E8
How many quaternions of soldiers was Paul delivered to?
(Acts 12:4)

For D6, A8, F3, B4
Of the cities given to the Levites, how many came from the half tribe of Manasseh? (Joshua 21:25)

For A1
How many times a day did David praise the Lord? (Psalm 119:164)

	A	B	C	D	E	F	G	H	I
1	■	■	■				■	■	■
2	■	■	■				■	■	■
3	■	■	■				■	■	■
4				■	■	■			
5				■	■	■			
6				■	■	■			
7	■	■	■				■	■	■
8	■	■	■				■	■	■
9	■	■	■				■	■	■

Starter Numbers in Order:
6, 8, 1, 3, 5, 9, 4, 2, 7

For D5, B6, H2, C3

In the first nine chapters of Numbers, which one contains the priests' blessing in verses 24–26?

For F4, D3, H1

According to Isaiah 19:18, how many cities in the land of Egypt would speak the language of Canaan?

For G2, B4, H7, F6

How many daughters did Leah have? (Genesis 34:1)

For F3, D6

How many days did the people of Jabesh-gilead fast for Saul and his sons? (1 Samuel 31:11–13)

For A3, H5, E2

How old was Josiah when he became king of Judah? (2 Kings 22:1)

For C4, H3, A2, B9, F1

How many thousand swine were choked in the sea? (Mark 5:13)

For H8, A9, I1, D2

How many days of pestilence did God send on Israel because of David's census? (2 Samuel 24:13–15)

For E9, C8

How many corners of the great sheet were knit? (Acts 10:11)

For D7, B1, E5, A4, G3

How many years did Hoshea reign? (2 Kings 17:1)

	A	B	C	D	E	F	G	H	I
1	▓	▓	▓				▓	▓	▓
2	▓	▓	▓				▓	▓	▓
3	▓	▓	▓				▓	▓	▓
4				▓	▓	▓			
5				▓	▓	▓			
6				▓	▓	▓			
7	▓	▓	▓				▓	▓	▓
8	▓	▓	▓				▓	▓	▓
9	▓	▓	▓				▓	▓	▓

Starter Numbers in Order:
6, 5, 1, 7, 8, 2, 3, 4, 9

For A1, I3, E5, F8, G9

How many times a day did Daniel's enemies accuse him of praying? (Daniel 6:13)

For B1, A4, G8, D9

How many cherubs were to be made on each end of the mercy seat? (Exodus 25:19)

For B2, C5, H6, A7, I9

How many stars were held by the One who addressed Sardis? (Revelation 3:1)

For C1, B4, H5, F6, I7

How many months did Benjamites, fleeing from Israel's army, stay at Rimmon's rock? (Judges 20:46–47)

For E2, D4, B5, C9

How many cities were given to the descendants of Aaron? (Joshua 21:13–16)

For F1, I2, C8

How many blind men sat by the wayside as Jesus passed through Jericho? (Matthew 20:29–30)

For G3, F9

How many years did young Joash stay hidden from his grandmother Athaliah at the temple of God? (2 Chronicles 22:10–12)

For H2, I4, E8

What number plus 30 was the number of years that the man by the Bethesda pool had an infirmity? (John 5:5)

For I1, F3, E4, D7, B9

How many sheep did Abigail, wife of the foolish Nabal, give to David and his men? (1 Samuel 25:18–20)

	A	B	C	D	E	F	G	H	I
1	▨	▨	▨				▨	▨	▨
2	▨	▨	▨				▨	▨	▨
3	▨	▨	▨				▨	▨	▨
4				▨	▨	▨			
5				▨	▨	▨			
6				▨	▨	▨			
7	▨	▨	▨				▨	▨	▨
8	▨	▨	▨				▨	▨	▨
9	▨	▨	▨				▨	▨	▨

Starter Numbers in Order:
3, 1, 7, 4, 9, 2, 6, 8, 5

For E7, B2, C4, I1

In the list of the Ten Commandments, what number commandment says, "Thou shalt not steal"? (Exodus 20:15)

For B9, H5, E1, I2

How many chapters are in the book of Amos?

For H2, A7, D8, B4, C1

How many times did Sanballat send messages to Nehemiah, asking if they could meet? (Nehemiah 6:5)

For I6

How many years was Abijam king of Judah? (1 Kings 15:1–2)

For D2, A3, I4, C7

How many days was the ancient feast described in Numbers 29:12?

For I8, E3, F5, A1

In the list of the plagues that God visited on Egypt, what number was frogs? (Exodus 8:1–15)

For F9, B1, H3, D5

In what year of Solomon's reign did he begin to build the house of the LORD? (1 Kings 6:1)

For D4, C6, E8, G1

How many chapters are in the book of 3 John?

For D1, G7, A2, B8, F4

How many waterpots were at the wedding at Cana? (John 2:1, 6)

	A	B	C	D	E	F	G	H	I
1	▓	▓	▓				▓	▓	▓
2	▓	▓	▓				▓	▓	▓
3	▓	▓	▓				▓	▓	▓
4				▓	▓	▓			
5				▓	▓	▓			
6				▓	▓	▓			
7	▓	▓	▓				▓	▓	▓
8	▓	▓	▓				▓	▓	▓
9	▓	▓	▓				▓	▓	▓

Starter Numbers in Order:
8, 9, 5, 3, 7, 2, 4, 1, 6

For D8, H2, C6

What number plus 9 equals the number of silver shekels that Jeremiah paid to buy the field at Anathoth? (Jeremiah 32:9)

For B4, G1, C8, E6

On the Day of Atonement, how many scapegoats were there? (Leviticus 16:8)

For H6, C2

All the days of Methuselah were _____ hundred and sixty-nine. (Genesis 5:27)

For H5, G7, F2, C3

How many days did Paul abide in Troas? (Acts 20:6)

For E8, G5, B3, F1

Which verse of Psalm 23 says that goodness and mercy will follow me all the days of my life?

For I6, A5

How many years was Pekahiah king of Israel? (2 Kings 15:23)

For F4, D9, A7, H8

How many gifts did the wise men bring to Jesus? (Matthew 2:11)

For D3, C1

How many smooth stones did David take? (1 Samuel 17:40)

For G4, E2, H1, C9, F8

How many men did Nebuchadnezzar see walking in the fire? (Daniel 3:25)

	A	B	C	D	E	F	G	H	I
1	░	░	░				░	░	░
2	░	░	░				░	░	░
3	░	░	░				░	░	░
4				░	░	░			
5				░	░	░			
6				░	░	░			
7	░	░	░				░	░	░
8	░	░	░				░	░	░
9	░	░	░				░	░	░

Starter Numbers in Order:
8, 1, 9, 7, 6, 2, 3, 5, 4

ANSWERS

1.

I	H	E	L	S	T	M	O	A
A	T	M	I	O	H	S	L	E
O	S	L	M	E	A	T	H	I
L	A	H	T	I	E	O	S	M
E	M	S	A	L	O	I	T	H
T	O	I	S	H	M	A	E	L
M	E	T	H	A	S	L	I	O
H	L	A	O	T	I	E	M	S
S	I	O	E	M	L	H	A	T

2.

9	5	7	4	3	2	1	6	8
6	2	4	1	7	8	9	3	5
1	3	8	6	5	9	4	7	2
4	1	9	3	8	7	5	2	6
7	8	2	5	4	6	3	1	9
5	6	3	2	9	1	7	8	4
8	7	6	9	1	4	2	5	3
3	9	1	8	2	5	6	4	7
2	4	5	7	6	3	8	9	1

3.

6	5	8	3	4	9	2	7	1
4	9	2	5	7	1	3	6	8
1	3	7	6	8	2	4	5	9
7	1	3	8	9	4	5	2	6
8	4	6	7	2	5	9	1	3
5	2	9	1	3	6	7	8	4
9	6	4	2	1	7	8	3	5
2	8	5	4	6	3	1	9	7
3	7	1	9	5	8	6	4	2

4.

4	8	5	1	2	9	6	7	3
6	2	7	5	4	3	8	9	1
9	1	3	6	7	8	4	5	2
3	5	4	7	9	6	1	2	8
7	6	1	3	8	2	9	4	5
8	9	2	4	1	5	7	3	6
5	4	8	9	3	1	2	6	7
1	7	6	2	5	4	3	8	9
2	3	9	8	6	7	5	1	4

5.

5	8	1	9	4	2	7	6	3
2	4	6	3	5	7	9	8	1
7	3	9	6	1	8	5	2	4
1	5	7	2	3	4	6	9	8
8	9	4	1	6	5	2	3	7
3	6	2	7	8	9	1	4	5
4	2	3	5	7	6	8	1	9
9	1	5	8	2	3	4	7	6
6	7	8	4	9	1	3	5	2

6.

8	3	5	6	1	4	2	9	7
7	2	6	8	3	9	1	4	5
4	1	9	2	7	5	6	3	8
5	4	1	3	2	8	7	6	9
2	8	7	5	9	6	4	1	3
9	6	3	7	4	1	5	8	2
1	9	2	4	5	3	8	7	6
6	5	4	9	8	7	3	2	1
3	7	8	1	6	2	9	5	4

ANSWERS

7.

6	7	3	8	4	5	2	1	9
1	8	9	3	6	2	4	7	5
2	4	5	7	1	9	3	6	8
4	2	6	1	3	8	9	5	7
3	1	8	9	5	7	6	2	4
5	9	7	4	2	6	8	3	1
8	3	1	2	7	4	5	9	6
7	6	4	5	9	3	1	8	2
9	5	2	6	8	1	7	4	3

8.

5	8	9	3	4	7	2	6	1
7	3	6	8	1	2	4	9	5
1	2	4	5	9	6	3	7	8
2	6	1	9	7	3	5	8	4
3	7	8	4	5	1	6	2	9
9	4	5	6	2	8	1	3	7
4	5	3	7	6	9	8	1	2
6	9	2	1	8	5	7	4	3
8	1	7	2	3	4	9	5	6

9.

6	9	2	5	7	1	4	3	8
4	7	1	6	8	3	5	9	2
5	3	8	9	2	4	1	7	6
7	5	9	4	1	2	6	8	3
2	4	6	3	9	8	7	1	5
8	1	3	7	5	6	2	4	9
9	2	5	8	4	7	3	6	1
1	6	4	2	3	9	8	5	7
3	8	7	1	6	5	9	2	4

10.

H	K	I	Y	O	M	E	N	L
O	M	L	N	E	I	Y	K	H
E	Y	N	H	K	L	I	M	O
L	N	H	M	Y	K	O	E	I
K	I	O	E	N	H	M	L	Y
M	E	Y	I	L	O	K	H	N
Y	O	E	K	H	N	L	I	M
N	L	M	O	I	E	H	Y	K
I	H	K	L	M	Y	N	O	E

11.

G	A	S	I	F	N	R	K	O
K	I	R	G	O	A	S	N	F
F	O	N	K	R	S	I	A	G
A	K	F	N	S	R	O	G	I
R	N	G	O	A	I	F	S	K
I	S	O	F	K	G	N	R	A
N	G	K	R	I	O	A	F	S
S	F	I	A	N	K	G	O	R
O	R	A	S	G	F	K	I	N

12.

7	8	1	4	6	2	3	5	9
3	6	4	5	1	9	7	2	8
2	9	5	3	8	7	4	6	1
8	1	6	7	9	4	2	3	5
4	5	2	6	3	1	8	9	7
9	7	3	2	5	8	6	1	4
1	2	9	8	4	3	5	7	6
5	3	8	9	7	6	1	4	2
6	4	7	1	2	5	9	8	3

ANSWERS

13.

8	3	5	6	7	2	4	1	9
7	2	9	3	4	1	6	8	5
1	6	4	9	8	5	7	3	2
6	4	8	5	9	3	1	2	7
3	9	1	7	2	4	8	5	6
5	7	2	1	6	8	9	4	3
2	1	6	8	5	7	3	9	4
9	5	3	4	1	6	2	7	8
4	8	7	2	3	9	5	6	1

14.

8	3	6	5	2	7	9	4	1
5	2	1	9	3	4	8	6	7
7	4	9	8	1	6	2	3	5
4	5	8	6	7	1	3	9	2
9	1	2	3	4	8	5	7	6
6	7	3	2	5	9	1	8	4
2	6	5	7	8	3	4	1	9
1	8	7	4	9	5	6	2	3
3	9	4	1	6	2	7	5	8

15.

6	5	2	1	3	4	7	8	9
8	4	1	9	2	7	6	5	3
9	7	3	5	6	8	1	4	2
1	9	7	6	8	3	5	2	4
5	6	4	2	1	9	8	3	7
2	3	8	4	7	5	9	1	6
7	2	9	8	4	1	3	6	5
3	8	6	7	5	2	4	9	1
4	1	5	3	9	6	2	7	8

16.

6	8	4	7	9	2	3	1	5
2	9	7	1	3	5	6	4	8
5	1	3	6	4	8	7	9	2
9	7	6	8	2	3	1	5	4
8	3	5	9	1	4	2	6	7
1	4	2	5	6	7	8	3	9
3	5	9	2	7	1	4	8	6
4	2	8	3	5	6	9	7	1
7	6	1	4	8	9	5	2	3

17.

5	1	9	8	7	4	6	2	3
3	8	4	1	6	2	9	7	5
2	7	6	5	9	3	4	1	8
6	4	2	3	8	9	1	5	7
8	9	5	7	4	1	3	6	2
7	3	1	2	5	6	8	9	4
1	5	8	9	3	7	2	4	6
9	6	3	4	2	5	7	8	1
4	2	7	6	1	8	5	3	9

18.

7	4	2	8	3	5	1	9	6
3	1	6	9	4	7	2	5	8
8	5	9	1	2	6	3	7	4
9	6	8	5	7	1	4	2	3
2	3	5	4	6	9	7	8	1
1	7	4	2	8	3	5	6	9
6	9	7	3	1	2	8	4	5
4	2	3	6	5	8	9	1	7
5	8	1	7	9	4	6	3	2

ANSWERS

19.

7	8	6	5	9	1	3	2	4
9	1	3	4	8	2	5	7	6
2	4	5	3	7	6	8	9	1
1	9	4	7	3	8	2	6	5
3	5	8	6	2	4	9	1	7
6	7	2	1	5	9	4	8	3
4	2	7	8	1	5	6	3	9
8	6	1	9	4	3	7	5	2
5	3	9	2	6	7	1	4	8

20.

E	S	P	D	G	O	R	A	I
D	I	R	P	S	A	O	G	E
G	O	A	I	R	E	S	D	P
A	R	I	S	D	P	G	E	O
O	G	S	E	A	R	I	P	D
P	D	E	O	I	G	A	S	R
S	E	G	R	P	I	D	O	A
R	A	O	G	E	D	P	I	S
I	P	D	A	O	S	E	R	G

21.

H	T	I	O	N	G	M	E	Y
O	G	N	Y	E	M	I	T	H
Y	E	M	I	T	H	G	O	N
G	N	T	E	I	Y	H	M	O
E	Y	H	N	M	O	T	I	G
M	I	O	H	G	T	Y	N	E
N	M	E	G	Y	I	O	H	T
I	O	G	T	H	E	N	Y	M
T	H	Y	M	O	N	E	G	I

22.

8	1	2	9	6	4	5	3	7
3	5	7	1	2	8	4	6	9
4	6	9	3	7	5	8	1	2
5	3	4	2	1	9	7	8	6
6	9	1	4	8	7	3	2	5
2	7	8	5	3	6	1	9	4
7	8	5	6	9	1	2	4	3
9	4	3	8	5	2	6	7	1
1	2	6	7	4	3	9	5	8

23.

6	1	8	3	7	5	2	9	4
5	7	2	9	4	1	3	6	8
9	3	4	8	6	2	1	7	5
3	4	7	1	9	8	6	5	2
1	6	5	2	3	4	9	8	7
8	2	9	6	5	7	4	3	1
7	8	6	4	2	3	5	1	9
2	9	1	5	8	6	7	4	3
4	5	3	7	1	9	8	2	6

24.

8	5	7	9	6	1	3	4	2
9	1	2	4	3	7	5	6	8
3	4	6	8	2	5	7	9	1
1	3	8	2	5	6	4	7	9
4	2	9	7	8	3	6	1	5
6	7	5	1	9	4	8	2	3
5	6	1	3	7	2	9	8	4
7	8	4	5	1	9	2	3	6
2	9	3	6	4	8	1	5	7

ANSWERS

25.

7	9	4	3	1	5	8	2	6
6	8	1	4	7	2	5	9	3
2	3	5	6	8	9	1	7	4
4	1	9	7	6	3	2	8	5
3	5	6	2	9	8	4	1	7
8	7	2	5	4	1	6	3	9
9	2	3	8	5	6	7	4	1
1	6	7	9	2	4	3	5	8
5	4	8	1	3	7	9	6	2

26.

7	1	4	9	2	6	8	3	5
9	3	2	7	8	5	6	1	4
5	6	8	1	3	4	9	7	2
2	7	5	8	9	1	3	4	6
8	9	6	4	5	3	7	2	1
1	4	3	2	6	7	5	8	9
4	5	9	3	7	2	1	6	8
3	8	1	6	4	9	2	5	7
6	2	7	5	1	8	4	9	3

27.

3	4	7	8	5	1	9	6	2
5	8	6	9	2	3	4	7	1
1	9	2	4	6	7	5	8	3
7	3	8	1	4	6	2	5	9
9	1	5	2	3	8	6	4	7
6	2	4	7	9	5	3	1	8
8	6	3	5	7	9	1	2	4
4	5	1	3	8	2	7	9	6
2	7	9	6	1	4	8	3	5

28.

2	5	7	3	6	8	4	9	1
4	6	8	5	1	9	3	7	2
9	1	3	4	7	2	5	8	6
6	4	9	7	5	3	1	2	8
1	7	5	2	8	4	6	3	9
3	8	2	6	9	1	7	4	5
5	3	1	8	2	7	9	6	4
7	2	6	9	4	5	8	1	3
8	9	4	1	3	6	2	5	7

29.

H	R	I	B	F	D	S	E	A
S	B	E	R	I	A	F	D	H
A	D	F	E	H	S	R	B	I
F	S	H	A	B	E	D	I	R
B	I	R	D	S	H	E	A	F
D	E	A	F	R	I	H	S	B
R	F	S	I	D	B	A	H	E
E	H	B	S	A	F	I	R	D
I	A	D	H	E	R	B	F	S

30.

T	R	H	S	O	N	I	B	E
I	S	E	R	B	T	H	O	N
B	O	N	E	H	I	S	R	T
S	T	I	H	R	E	B	N	O
O	E	R	B	N	S	T	I	H
H	N	B	I	T	O	E	S	R
N	I	S	O	E	H	R	T	B
E	B	O	T	S	R	N	H	I
R	H	T	N	I	B	O	E	S

ANSWERS

31.

3	7	4	9	8	1	5	2	6
2	5	9	3	7	6	4	8	1
6	1	8	5	2	4	9	7	3
5	6	7	4	9	3	2	1	8
8	2	1	6	5	7	3	4	9
9	4	3	8	1	2	7	6	5
1	9	6	2	4	5	8	3	7
7	8	2	1	3	9	6	5	4
4	3	5	7	6	8	1	9	2

32.

7	8	1	5	9	3	4	2	6
5	3	2	4	7	6	9	8	1
6	4	9	1	2	8	3	7	5
4	1	7	8	6	5	2	9	3
8	9	5	3	1	2	7	6	4
3	2	6	7	4	9	1	5	8
9	6	3	2	5	1	8	4	7
1	5	4	9	8	7	6	3	2
2	7	8	6	3	4	5	1	9

33.

3	7	8	9	5	4	6	1	2
9	1	2	6	7	3	8	4	5
4	5	6	1	8	2	9	3	7
5	8	1	7	9	6	4	2	3
2	9	4	8	3	5	1	7	6
7	6	3	2	4	1	5	8	9
6	3	7	5	1	8	2	9	4
8	4	5	3	2	9	7	6	1
1	2	9	4	6	7	3	5	8

34.

8	1	5	3	4	6	9	2	7
9	3	6	8	2	7	1	4	5
2	7	4	9	1	5	3	6	8
3	4	8	1	5	9	2	7	6
5	9	7	2	6	3	4	8	1
1	6	2	4	7	8	5	9	3
6	8	9	5	3	2	7	1	4
4	2	3	7	8	1	6	5	9
7	5	1	6	9	4	8	3	2

35.

4	6	3	5	2	7	1	8	9
9	1	2	3	6	8	4	5	7
7	8	5	9	1	4	2	3	6
1	5	9	7	4	3	6	2	8
2	3	7	8	9	6	5	4	1
8	4	6	2	5	1	7	9	3
3	9	4	1	7	2	8	6	5
5	2	1	6	8	9	3	7	4
6	7	8	4	3	5	9	1	2

36.

4	5	8	6	3	1	9	7	2
6	9	3	7	2	4	1	8	5
1	7	2	8	5	9	3	4	6
8	1	4	3	9	6	2	5	7
5	2	6	1	7	8	4	9	3
7	3	9	2	4	5	6	1	8
2	4	7	9	8	3	5	6	1
9	8	1	5	6	2	7	3	4
3	6	5	4	1	7	8	2	9

ANSWERS

37.

5	9	6	8	1	2	7	3	4
7	2	8	3	4	6	1	5	9
1	3	4	5	7	9	8	2	6
6	4	5	7	8	3	9	1	2
8	1	2	9	5	4	3	6	7
9	7	3	2	6	1	4	8	5
2	6	1	4	9	8	5	7	3
3	5	9	1	2	7	6	4	8
4	8	7	6	3	5	2	9	1

38.

R	O	S	C	H	I	N	T	A
I	C	A	T	R	N	S	H	O
N	H	T	O	A	S	C	R	I
A	N	O	S	T	R	I	C	H
S	R	H	I	O	C	A	N	T
C	T	I	H	N	A	O	S	R
H	I	N	A	C	T	R	O	S
O	S	R	N	I	H	T	A	C
T	A	C	R	S	O	H	I	N

39.

T	H	E	L	O	W	I	N	G
I	L	O	E	N	G	W	H	T
N	W	G	I	H	T	L	O	E
H	I	N	W	E	O	T	G	L
W	E	T	H	G	L	O	I	N
G	O	L	N	T	I	H	E	W
L	G	I	O	W	N	E	T	H
E	N	W	T	I	H	G	L	O
O	T	H	G	L	E	N	W	I

40.

9	5	6	8	1	7	3	4	2
7	8	1	4	2	3	5	6	9
4	2	3	9	5	6	7	8	1
1	9	2	3	4	5	8	7	6
8	3	4	6	7	2	9	1	5
5	6	7	1	8	9	4	2	3
6	7	9	2	3	4	1	5	8
2	1	5	7	9	8	6	3	4
3	4	8	5	6	1	2	9	7

41.

6	7	2	4	1	8	5	9	3
8	4	9	3	6	5	2	7	1
1	3	5	7	9	2	4	8	6
9	6	8	5	7	4	3	1	2
2	5	7	8	3	1	6	4	9
3	1	4	9	2	6	7	5	8
4	9	6	1	5	3	8	2	7
5	2	1	6	8	7	9	3	4
7	8	3	2	4	9	1	6	5

42.

7	9	1	2	4	6	8	3	5
8	2	6	7	5	3	4	9	1
4	3	5	9	8	1	2	6	7
6	1	4	3	2	7	9	5	8
9	8	2	5	6	4	7	1	3
5	7	3	8	1	9	6	4	2
1	5	7	4	9	8	3	2	6
2	4	8	6	3	5	1	7	9
3	6	9	1	7	2	5	8	4

ANSWERS

43.

7	5	2	4	6	3	9	1	8
4	8	6	1	2	9	7	3	5
1	9	3	7	5	8	2	4	6
5	4	8	9	7	1	3	6	2
9	6	7	2	3	5	4	8	1
2	3	1	6	8	4	5	7	9
3	2	9	8	4	6	1	5	7
6	7	5	3	1	2	8	9	4
8	1	4	5	9	7	6	2	3

44.

5	2	3	7	6	4	1	8	9
4	8	6	3	1	9	2	5	7
7	9	1	2	8	5	6	3	4
6	7	9	5	3	8	4	1	2
8	1	5	6	4	2	9	7	3
3	4	2	9	7	1	5	6	8
2	3	8	4	5	6	7	9	1
9	5	7	1	2	3	8	4	6
1	6	4	8	9	7	3	2	5

45.

3	8	5	6	9	2	7	1	4
7	4	9	3	1	8	2	6	5
2	1	6	5	4	7	3	8	9
5	6	7	2	8	4	9	3	1
8	3	2	1	5	9	6	4	7
1	9	4	7	3	6	5	2	8
9	7	1	4	2	3	8	5	6
6	5	3	8	7	1	4	9	2
4	2	8	9	6	5	1	7	3

46.

6	9	4	3	7	2	8	1	5
7	5	1	4	8	6	9	2	3
8	2	3	1	9	5	4	6	7
9	3	6	5	1	7	2	4	8
2	4	5	6	3	8	1	7	9
1	7	8	2	4	9	3	5	6
5	8	9	7	2	1	6	3	4
3	1	7	8	6	4	5	9	2
4	6	2	9	5	3	7	8	1

47.

1	3	6	8	2	7	5	4	9
9	4	7	1	3	5	2	6	8
2	5	8	9	6	4	1	3	7
3	8	4	7	9	1	6	5	2
5	1	9	6	8	2	3	7	4
6	7	2	5	4	3	8	9	1
4	9	3	2	1	6	7	8	5
7	6	1	4	5	8	9	2	3
8	2	5	3	7	9	4	1	6

48.

G	S	I	O	T	U	H	E	R
R	H	U	G	E	S	O	T	I
T	O	E	R	I	H	S	U	G
I	T	S	E	R	G	U	O	H
H	E	R	U	S	O	I	G	T
U	G	O	T	H	I	R	S	E
E	U	H	S	G	R	T	I	O
S	R	G	I	O	T	E	H	U
O	I	T	H	U	E	G	R	S

ANSWERS

49.

R	F	C	L	I	E	A	M	U
M	A	L	C	F	U	I	R	E
E	I	U	M	A	R	L	F	C
C	L	F	U	E	A	R	I	M
A	M	E	R	C	I	F	U	L
U	R	I	F	M	L	C	E	A
L	C	R	I	U	M	E	A	F
F	U	A	E	R	C	M	L	I
I	E	M	A	L	F	U	C	R

50.

7	8	4	1	9	5	2	3	6
9	1	2	4	6	3	5	7	8
3	5	6	7	8	2	9	1	4
6	2	7	8	3	9	1	4	5
8	9	1	5	7	4	3	6	2
4	3	5	2	1	6	7	8	9
1	6	8	9	5	7	4	2	3
2	7	9	3	4	8	6	5	1
5	4	3	6	2	1	8	9	7

51.

7	9	1	4	6	2	8	5	3
2	4	5	3	8	9	1	6	7
8	3	6	5	1	7	9	2	4
9	1	2	8	3	5	7	4	6
5	7	3	6	9	4	2	8	1
4	6	8	7	2	1	3	9	5
6	8	7	9	5	3	4	1	2
1	5	4	2	7	8	6	3	9
3	2	9	1	4	6	5	7	8

52.

3	1	4	8	6	2	7	9	5
6	7	5	3	9	1	4	8	2
9	2	8	4	7	5	6	1	3
1	4	6	9	5	7	2	3	8
2	9	7	6	3	8	5	4	1
5	8	3	2	1	4	9	7	6
7	3	1	5	2	9	8	6	4
4	6	2	7	8	3	1	5	9
8	5	9	1	4	6	3	2	7

53.

2	4	5	6	9	3	1	7	8
6	8	3	7	4	1	2	5	9
7	1	9	8	2	5	3	4	6
9	5	8	1	3	6	4	2	7
3	7	6	4	5	2	8	9	1
4	2	1	9	7	8	5	6	3
5	3	7	2	8	9	6	1	4
8	6	4	5	1	7	9	3	2
1	9	2	3	6	4	7	8	5

54.

8	2	5	9	3	6	1	4	7
1	3	9	2	4	7	5	8	6
4	6	7	5	8	1	9	2	3
9	1	6	7	2	3	4	5	8
2	5	3	4	9	8	6	7	1
7	4	8	6	1	5	3	9	2
3	8	2	1	5	9	7	6	4
5	7	1	8	6	4	2	3	9
6	9	4	3	7	2	8	1	5

MORE GREAT LARGE PRINT PUZZLES!

Bible Memory Crosswords Large Print

Here's a collection of crosswords sure to satisfy. The "clue" for each puzzle is a memory verse, with several key words missing—you'll need to remember (or look up) those missing words to plug them into the puzzle grid.

Paperback / 978-1-63609-105-1 / $6.99

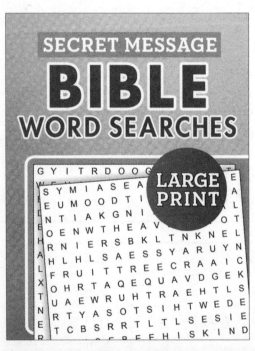

Secret Message Bible Word Searches Large Print

These large print puzzles provide a brief passage with search words highlighted. When the puzzle is solved, there's a special bonus: The leftover letters spell out a "secret message," a Bible trivia question related to the puzzle theme!

Paperback / 978-1-64352-030-8 / $6.99